United We Stand

The War on Terrorism

By Nancy Louis

Visit us at
www.abdopub.com

Edited by Paul Joseph
Graphic Design: John Hamilton
Cover Design: Mighty Media
Photos: AP/Wide World

Library of Congress Cataloging-in-Publication Data

Louis, Nancy, 1952-
United we stand / Nancy Louis.
p. cm. — (War on terrorism)
Includes index.
Summary: Describes many of the things corporations and individuals did to help, both in the United States and in other countries, after the terrorist attacks of September 11, such as donating money, blood, food, and supplies, creating memorials, and volunteering in various capacities.
ISBN 1-57765-660-1
1. September 11 Terrorist Attacks, 2001—Juvenile literature. 2. Victims of terrorism—Services for—United States—Juvenile literature. 3. Disaster relief—United States—Juvenile literature. 4. Charities—United States—Juvenile literature. 5. Voluntarism—United States—Juvenile literature. 6. Helping behavior—United States—Juvenile literature. [1. September 11 Terrorist Attacks, 2001. 2. Voluntarism.] I. Title. II. Series.

HV6432 .L69 2002
973.931—d21

2001058956

Table of Contents

Americans Come Together 5

A Call For Help 7

Young People Help 11

New York Rallies 15

A United Country 19

The World Responds 23

Making A Difference 27

Celebrity Contributions 31

We Will Always Remember 37

How You Can Help 43

Timeline 44

Where On The Web? 45

Glossary 46

Index.. 48

Rainbow 16.95

4-02

Showing The Colors

A Boy Scout waves the American flag during a prayer service at Yankee Stadium in New York, September 23, 2001.

Americans Come Together

AFTER THE TERRORIST ATTACKS OF September 11, 2001, many Americans felt a renewed sense of patriotism and unity. The song "God Bless America," by Irving Berlin, was played repeatedly throughout the United States. The lyrics are simple, direct, and send a strong message.

Americans proudly displayed their patriotism and unity. The American flag flew at businesses and homes all across the country. People wore flag pins on their lapels, and red, white, and blue clothing. Store windows displayed flags. People placed flag decals and bumper stickers on their cars. The flag carried a message of healing in a time of sadness, loss, and fear.

People in the United States and around the world came together and answered the call for help. They showed their compassion and generosity to the people most affected by the attacks.

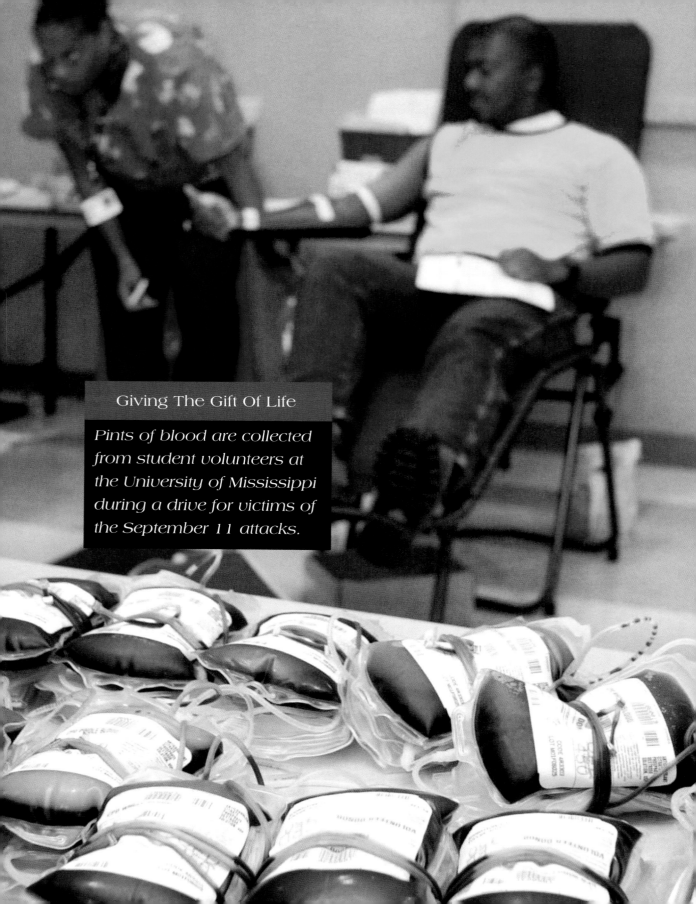

Giving The Gift Of Life

Pints of blood are collected from student volunteers at the University of Mississippi during a drive for victims of the September 11 attacks.

A Call For Help

THE MAIN ROLE OF MANY NONPROFIT organizations and charities is to help people and communities in times of need. After the September 11 terrorist attacks, hundreds of organizations offered their help. They aided in search-and-rescue operations, raised money to help the families of the victims, and sent emergency disaster supplies.

People throughout the country came together to donate blood, money, and time. The response was overwhelming. In New York, people waited up to three hours to donate blood. In other areas of the country, people lined up at blood banks and mobile stations to do what they could to help.

In one week, the Red Cross raised more than $128 million. Of this, more than $36 million came through its Web site. Major corporations also donated millions of dollars to the Red Cross.

The Salvation Army organized relief efforts for the attack victims and their families. It served more than 100,000 meals a day to rescue-and-recovery workers at Ground Zero. It also collected supplies and materials. Cash donations helped the Salvation Army quickly send supplies to where they were needed most.

Immediately following the attacks, the United Way of New York and the New York Community Trust established the September 11th Fund. Many corporations and foundations donated to the fund. The money will serve the needs of the

Collecting Donations

Eryn Norton, 11, left, and Erin Chaiken, 9, collect money as they raise donations for the Red Cross in Dallas, Texas.

victims, their families, and all those affected by the tragedy. Microsoft Corporation pledged $10 million to the September 11th Fund. The Lilly Endowment donated $10 million to the short- and long-term needs of individuals and communities in crisis from the attacks.

Cross-Cultural Solutions, a nonprofit group, organized volunteers to serve food aboard the *Spirit of New York* to rescue workers. This cruise ship, docked at the World Financial Center, was transformed into a 24-hour respite center for the thousands of workers at Ground Zero. Volunteers provided about 10,000 meals daily. There was a waiting list of more than 700 people who wanted to volunteer their time.

American Forests, a nonprofit organization, plants and cares for trees in cities to improve the environment and restore the Earth. The attack on America compelled the organization to plant trees in cities across the country. These memorials commemorate the victims and the heroes. They also honor America and its future.

Amazon.com, AOL Time Warner, Microsoft, Yahoo, Cisco Systems, and eBay sponsored the American Liberty Partnership. The alliance was formed to facilitate rapid response, provide accurate and up-to-date information, and collect contributions. Sponsors used their Web sites to raise money. For example, eBay's Auction for America hoped to raise $100 million in 100 days. Microsoft pledged $5 million in technical support, volunteer hours, and software to aid the recovery effort and other organizations serving people in the affected area.

WHITE KNOLL
MIDDLE SCHOOL

WAR HAWKS

Kindness Repaid

White Knoll Middle School student Russell Hall, right, shakes hands with New York City firefighters during a ceremony at the school in West Columbia, South Carolina, on December 5, 2001. The firefighters thanked the students for raising money to replace one of many fire trucks lost in the terrorist attacks.

Young People Help

THE ATTACK ON AMERICA AFFECTED MILLIONS of people, young and old. Many lost family members, friends, and acquaintances. Across the country, young people found ways to make a difference.

Students at White Knoll Middle School in Columbia, South Carolina, raised almost a half million dollars to buy a fire truck for New York City. The donation repaid an 1867 debt Columbia owed to New York City.

White Knoll Principal Nancy Turner learned about the debt from Columbia's fire chief, John D. Jansen. Jansen explained that at the close of the Civil War, New York City firefighters made a peace offering to Columbia. They sent a fire wagon to Columbia, which had burned two years earlier. Columbia vowed to someday repay the debt.

A New York attorney originally from South Carolina helped by pledging $100,000 towards the cost of the new truck. State Education Superintendent Inez Tenenbaum said, "This is the ultimate example of character education. These students have given a gift to the people of New York, but they have also given a gift to all of us."

Students of Oceanside Middle School in New York answered President Bush's call for children in the United States to help the children of Afghanistan by donating dollar bills to America's Fund for Afghan Children. They created an eight-foot (two-m) tall "giving tree" in the school's lobby. Students covered the tree with dollar bills. Their goal was to raise $1,000 to aid Afghan children. One student commented that it was hard to imagine how it felt to be trapped in a country where there was no safe place to be, no food, and no one to help them.

Teens Improving New York (TINY) was started by Abena Mackall, Niki Achitoff-Gray, Julia Baskin, and Jack Kirkland. The four were freshmen at Stuyvesant High School, located a few blocks from the World Trade Center. The school was immediately evacuated after the first plane hit the North Tower. For the next week, it was used as a relief center for police officers, firefighters, and rescue workers. The group offered its assistance to the Red Cross, but was turned away because there were so many volunteers. To raise money, they decided to bake cookies, brownies, and cupcakes and hold a bake sale. They set up a folding table near a record store on a busy Manhattan street and asked for donations. In a few hours, TINY raised more than $600 for the *New York Times* 9/11 Neediest Fund.

Three New York teenagers, Taina Rodriguez, Victor Alvarez, and his twin sister, Veronica, were kindergartners in 1993. They were on a school trip to the World Trade Center when a bomb exploded in the basement. After the explosion, Tania was stuck in an elevator for eight hours. Victor had to walk down 107 floors in the dark and cold. It took him 12 hours to reach the first floor. Veronica made it down to ground level safely without incident.

The September 11 attack brought back frightening memories for them. Taina, Victor, and Veronica decided to honor those who lost their lives in the attack. They made pins from red, white, and blue ribbons, plastic peace doves, praying hands, and American flags. They raised $1,000, which they donated to the Red Cross.

Six students from Binghamton, New York, gave 1,200 teddy bears to the families of police officers and firefighters who lost their lives in the attack. Each bear was individually wrapped with a special note from the class. They personally delivered the bears to several fire stations near Ground Zero. They also donated some of the bears to displaced students in lower Manhattan.

Ribbons Of Love

From left, Veronica Alvarez, Taina Rodriguez, and Victor Alvarez make ribbons to raise money for victims of the terrorist attacks.

Generous Donations

A woman attaches a donation to a replica of the Statue of Liberty. A New York restaurant used the money to help feed workers at Ground Zero.

New York Rallies

FOLLOWING THE ATTACK, THE PEOPLE OF NEW York came together to get through the tragedy. Restaurants gave away free food. Grocery stores handed out flashlights and other supplies. Medical students volunteered at hospitals. Members of local churches handed out water. Thousands of people donated blood, clothing, and supplies. Two women offered their apartment to anyone who needed a shower or wanted to make a phone call. Others opened their homes to those who had no place to go.

Many special funds were created just to support New York's victims and their families. The Twin Towers Fund was set up to assist, support, and recognize the families of uniformed service members, such as New York City firefighters, police officers, Emergency Medical Services Command, and the Port Authority of New York and New Jersey. The International Association of Fire Fighters created The New York Firefighters 9-11 Disaster Relief Fund. This fund ensures that the families of fallen firefighters get the assistance they need. The State of New York set up the World Trade Center Relief Fund to aid the families of those who were injured and those who died.

Governor George Pataki announced a scholarship program for the victims' families. The scholarship applies to tuition, fees, room, board, and transportation at the State University of New York and the City University of New York. Mayor Rudolph Giuliani felt this was a way to ensure that the families of the firefighters, police officers, rescue workers, and emergency medical personnel will not need to worry about their children's future.

September 11th Fund

Two men unload more than 18,000 checks from the September 11th Fund for people who were injured or lost loved ones in the terrorist attacks.

Stepping Up To The Plate

New York Mayor Rudolph Giuliani accepts a Louisville Slugger baseball bat from Louisville, Kentucky, Mayor David Armstrong, who also presented Giuliani with a $1.4 million check for charities serving victims of the September 11 attacks.

Candlelight Vigil

Over 10,000 people attended a candle ceremony in Madison, Wisconsin, on September 14, 2001. It was just one of many held around the country in memory of the victims of the September 11 attacks.

A United Country

FEW EVENTS IN HISTORY HAVE BROUGHT THE country together as did the events of September 11, 2001. The U.S. government focused on helping the nation heal after the terrorist attacks.

Congress unanimously passed a $40 billion emergency spending package three days after the attacks. Most of the money was spent on recovery and cleanup at the sites of the plane crashes. The rest of the funds were to be spent on intelligence, law enforcement, and improved federal security.

Congress also introduced legislation to issue war bonds from the Department of the Treasury. War bonds allow citizens to give loans to the U.S. government, which are later repaid. Purchasing war bonds is a way to contribute directly to the fight against terrorism.

President Bush asked each American child to help the children in Afghanistan by donating one dollar to America's Fund for Afghan Children. The fund aids the more than 10 million Afghan children who have suffered from years of war, drought, and the harsh Taliban government. America is focused on eliminating terrorism, but it is also concerned about the well-being of innocent people in Afghanistan.

An email pen pal program called Friendship Through Education was created to help young people learn tolerance and understand cultural differences. It pairs American students with Muslim students in Arab countries. President Bush said the best way to fight fear is with friendship and hope. He went on to say that it is important for people who practice Islam to know that America does not hold them responsible for the terrorist attacks. Three schools located near the crash sites in New York City and Washington, D.C., were chosen to begin the program. Students at these schools will be writing to students in Bahrain, Pakistan, and Egypt.

The U.S. Postal Service unveiled a new patriotic postage stamp called United We Stand three weeks after the terrorist attacks. Postmaster General John E. Potter explained that the first-class stamp represents America's core values of freedom, liberty, and justice. It is a reminder to the world that America will not be defeated by terrorism.

On October 2, 2001, the U.S. Postal Service unveiled the new 34-cent "United We Stand" American flag stamp. The Postal Service was flooded with calls for a new patriotic stamp following the terrorist attacks of September 11.

Memorial To Fallen Heroes

A makeshift memorial filled with candles and a 13-star flag sits in Brooklyn, New York, across the river from the site of the terrorist attacks on the World Trade Center.

In Memory Of Loved Ones

A U.S. Marine guard looks at the floral tributes outside the U.S. Embassy in London in memory of the victims of the September 11 terrorist attacks.

The World Responds

ACROSS AMERICA, AND AROUND THE world, people wanted to help in any way they could. Many were far from the attack areas but wanted to do something to help. It was a time to put aside differences and come together to aid fellow citizens. Communities around the world reached out to help.

Students at colleges and universities everywhere held candlelight vigils. Religious groups offered prayer and counseling. Children in a Chicago suburb inspired their whole community to participate in a garage sale. They sold toys, games, and books to raise money.

Students in Fort Myers, Florida, contributed by working with local grocery stores. The students decorated paper bags with patriotic pictures and messages. The bags were returned to the stores and used to bag groceries.

The city of Las Vegas, Nevada, dedicated the Police Memorial Park to the fallen officers of the September 11 tragedy. Family members of officers who died in the line of duty were given the opportunity to plant trees in memory of their loved ones.

Around the world, countries shared America's grief. Many citizens from other countries died in the terrorist attacks. Countries showed their support and solidarity in many ways.

In Hungary, firefighters hung black ribbons on firetrucks in memory of the New York firefighters who lost their lives in the attacks. Russia and NATO sent a joint statement denouncing the attacks on America.

Japan and Pakistan promised full cooperation in efforts to fight terrorism. European Union foreign ministers offered immediate search-and-rescue help. Former and current U.S. adversaries Syria, Cuba, Libya, and Iran expressed their support.

Israel and France condemned the attacks and vowed to help in any way needed. Italy flew its flags at half-mast to show solidarity for democracy and freedom. Pope John Paul II sent a telegram to President Bush, declaring his deep sorrow and prayer in this dark time.

Canadians Care, a nonprofit organization, raised money for friends and families of the victims of the World Trade Center attack. All of the money received was donated to relief assistance. Many Canadians died in the attacks. The organization reminded the world that the United States is not alone in the tragedy.

"Canada Loves New York" weekend, November 30 to December 2, 2001, was an opportunity for Canadians to visit New York City and attend an inspiring rally. Special airline and hotel rates were offered so Canadians could make it to the rally and visit the city of New York.

Although the British Red Cross could not donate blood due to the fear of contamination, thousands of messages of sympathy and support were transmitted through the U.S. Embassy. Cash contributions were collected and forwarded to the American Red

Cross to aid its New York relief effort. Great Britain also played the United States national anthem during the changing of the guards at Buckingham Palace in London in memory of the victims of September 11.

Sheikh Mohammed al Maktoum, crown prince of Dubai and defense minister of the United Arab Emirates, made a $5 million contribution to the Red Cross.

FOR ALL THE CHILDREN WHO WERE ONCE AGAIN INNOCENT VICTIMS

The U.S. Is Not Alone

A young girl places a candle outside the U.S. Embassy in Ottawa, Canada.

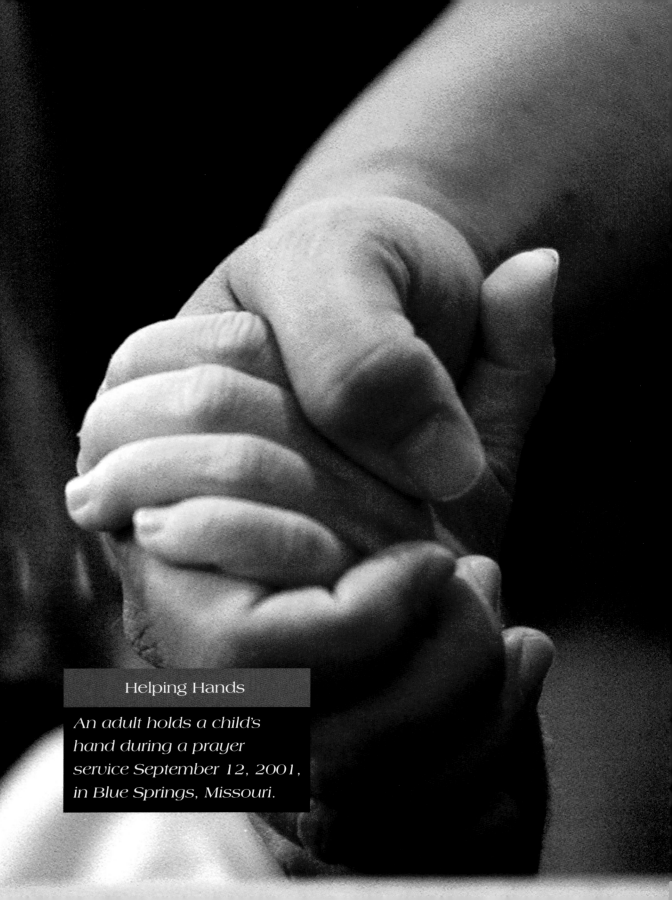

Helping Hands

An adult holds a child's hand during a prayer service September 12, 2001, in Blue Springs, Missouri.

Making A Difference

A CROSS THE NATION, INDIVIDUALS DID what they could to help heal the country and support democracy. Thomas Kinkade, a well-known artist, created a limited-edition painting in memory of September 11, 2001. The title of the work is *The Light of Freedom*. The profits from the sale of the painting went to the Salvation Army. Kinkade described the painting as "symbolic of our nation and inspired by God."

Two women in Prescott Valley, Arizona, who wanted to do something to honor those who lost their lives on September 11, made the WTC Memorial Quilt. The individual blocks of the quilt were created for specific groups, such as the World Trade Center victims, Pentagon victims, all hijacked plane crews and passengers, rescue workers, firefighters, police officers, and other victims. Family members of victims helped make the blocks. More than 1,000 volunteers worked on the project. The completed quilt was donated to the American people. The U.S. government will display it in cities across the country as a tribute to all those who died.

Flag Across America

A group of pilots and volunteers run near Fredericksburg, Virginia, during a leg of "Flag Across America."

Hundreds of United and American airlines employees organized a coast-to-coast marathon, "Flag Across America," in memory of the crews and passengers who died. They retraced the scheduled routes of Flights 11 and 175, leaving Boston for Los Angeles. The runners carried an American flag in a relay through New York, Washington, D.C., Atlanta, Dallas, Oklahoma City, Albuquerque, and Phoenix. The relay ended at Los Angeles International Airport. The airline employees honored their fallen comrades by showing their patriotism and raising money for the families of the victims.

Five firefighters who lived through the disaster biked across the country on a memorial "Thank You America" tour. The month-long trip began at Ground Zero and ended in Los Angeles. They rode customized red, white, and blue ergonomic bicycles supplied by Cannondale, a top bicycle manufacturer. The riders visited about 100 firehouses along the way. Each firefighter carried mementos of their fallen comrades. They paid their own expenses except for their flights back home from Los Angeles, which were donated by United and American airlines.

In Minneapolis, Minnesota, Joe Temeczko willed his entire estate to the people of New York. Temeczko immigrated to the United States from Poland through Ellis Island in 1950. He told friends and neighbors he felt a connection to New York because people there were good to him. Temeczko was a self-employed laborer and a junk collector. Joe spent his time retrieving furniture, electronics, tools, and toys from neighborhood dumpsters. He fixed the broken items he found and sold them. Joe died at age 86. Few people knew he had an estate worth more than $1 million.

Other contributions came from various sources that showed the compassion people felt nationwide. Grocery store chain Stop & Shop matched contributions from customers and associates in a fundraising program for victims and their families. The Knights of Columbus donated $1 million to families of victims lost on September 11, 2001.

KMBC-TV in Kansas City joined the Red Cross in a telethon. Workers took pledges and donations for victims in the attack on America. The event raised over $500,000 for relief efforts in New York and Washington, D.C. A fund drive organized by a New Orleans TV station raised $300,000 in cash contributions for the relief effort in less than 24 hours.

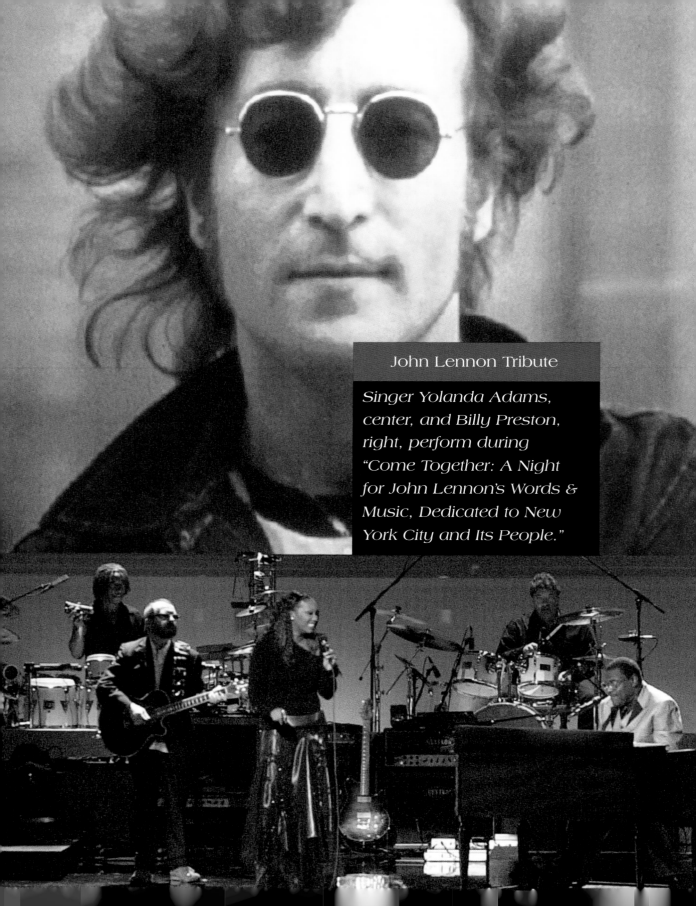

John Lennon Tribute

Singer Yolanda Adams, center, and Billy Preston, right, perform during "Come Together: A Night for John Lennon's Words & Music, Dedicated to New York City and Its People."

Celebrity Contributions

ELEBRITIES ORGANIZED BENEFITS AS A WAY of helping others and healing a wounded nation. The first large-scale event was the *America: A Tribute to Heroes* telethon. It aired on 30 television networks, 8,000 radio stations, and the Internet. It raised more than $150 million in pledges. Tom Hanks, Goldie Hawn, Robin Williams, Julia Roberts, Tom Cruise, and George Clooney were just a few of the stars who donated their time and talent to the cause. All of the performers, stagehands, and organizers worked without pay.

A televised tribute to the late John Lennon was dedicated to New York City and its people. More than a dozen performers, including Dave Matthews, Marc Anthony, Natalie Merchant, and Cyndi Lauper, gathered to play such Lennon songs as "Give Peace a Chance," "Imagine," "Come Together," and "Power to the People." Yoko Ono, Lennon's widow, thanked the firefighters, police officers, and rescue workers for their heroism and bravery during the terrorist attacks. She told them, "You have restored my faith in the human race."

"Stand Up for New York" was a benefit at Carnegie Hall hosted by leading comedians, including Jerry Seinfeld, Bill Cosby, Colin Quinn, Will Ferrell, and George Wallace. The money raised from the event went to the Twin Towers Fund and the New York Police and Fire Widow and Children Benefit Fund.

Paul McCartney released a new song called "From a Lover to a Friend" as a tribute to all those who lost their lives on September 11. Money from the sales of the single will go to the New York Fire and Police Departments. At the time of the attack, McCartney was on a plane in New York waiting to take off. He saw the final moments of the twin towers from his window. McCartney stayed in New York for a week after the attack. He witnessed firsthand the heroism and bravery of so many who came to Ground Zero to help. His father had been a volunteer fireman in Liverpool during World War II, so he particularly empathized with the firefighters.

McCartney teamed up with other musicians to organize "Concert for the Americas" on October 20, 2001, from Madison Square Garden. Stages in New York, Los Angeles, and London hosted musicians such as Bon Jovi, Elton John, Mick Jagger, Eric Clapton, and The Who. The concert was a show of support for democracy and freedom in the face of tragedy.

Many musicians, actresses, and actors gave their time, talent, and money. The Backstreet Boys and Lynrd Skynrd each donated $10,000 from ticket sales during their concert tours. Britney Spears donated one dollar from every ticket during her U.S. tour. Millions of dollars went to the children of New York firefighters.

Benefit Concert

Paul McCartney performs at the "Concert for the Americas" benefit at Madison Square Garden on October 20, 2001.

"What More Can I Give?"

Michael Jackson performs at the "United We Stand: What More Can I Give?" benefit concert October 21, 2001, at RFK Stadium in Washington, D.C.

Rosie O'Donnell, Sandra Bullock, Jim Carey, and Dr. Dre each made a $1 million contribution. Julia Roberts contributed $1 million to the American Red Cross and $1 million to the September 11 Telethon Fund. Diana Ross, Patti Labelle, Queen Latifah, and other female recording artists re-recorded Sister Sledge's song, "We Are Family," to aid charities supporting victims of the attacks. Michael Jackson recorded a new song called, "What More Can I Give?" The sales are expected to raise $50 million for relief efforts. Willie Nelson proclaimed that his Farm Aid 2001 concert profits would go to restore farmers' markets destroyed in the World Trade Center attack.

Those in the sports world also helped out. Each school in the college football Southeastern, Big 12, and Big Ten Conferences donated $1 million from ticket sales and television fees to aid victims of the attack. The NFL and the player associations placed at least $5 million each in a special relief fund. Grants were made available immediately to aid firefighters, police officers, emergency personnel, and volunteers. The NBA players, teams, and owners provided more that $2 million in cash donations and supplies.

Sports figures such as Tiger Woods, Andre Agassi, Lindsay Davenport, Pete Sampras, and Venus and Serena Williams donated prized memorabilia to Auction for America, an Internet auction on eBay. Sports fans also participated by donating such items as a basketball signed by Shaquille O'Neal and a baseball autographed by Yogi Berra.

Showing Support

Ricky Roman holds his daughter, Jeanelle, 5, during a candlelight vigil to show support for victims of the September 11 attacks.

We Will Always Remember

ACROSS THE UNITED STATES AND AROUND the world, people organized vigils following the terrorist attacks. Parks, neighborhoods, schools, and businesses observed times of silence and prayer for those who survived and those who lost their lives. In remembrance, people raised flags, lit candles, and sang songs. People of different cultures and religions came together to honor those heroes who died or suffered in the attacks.

President Bush declared September 14, 2001, a national day of prayer and remembrance. He asked the country to come together at lunchtime for a moment of silence and prayer. That evening, thousands attended a candlelight vigil held at Union Square in Manhattan.

In Europe, September 15, 2001, was declared a day of mourning. At 11 A.M., more than 800 million people in 43 countries observed three minutes of silence in memory of the attacks on America. Memorial services in churches and government offices honored the victims and their families.

Marking the one-month anniversary of the deadly attacks, recovery workers paused for a memorial service at Ground Zero. As bagpipes played, the New York Fire Department's new chaplain, Rabbi Joseph Potasnik, Police Chaplain Monsignor David Cassato, and Mayor Rudolph Giuliani presided over the service. Potasnik encouraged those at the service to look at the dedication, not the destruction, and focus on the heroism, not the terrorism.

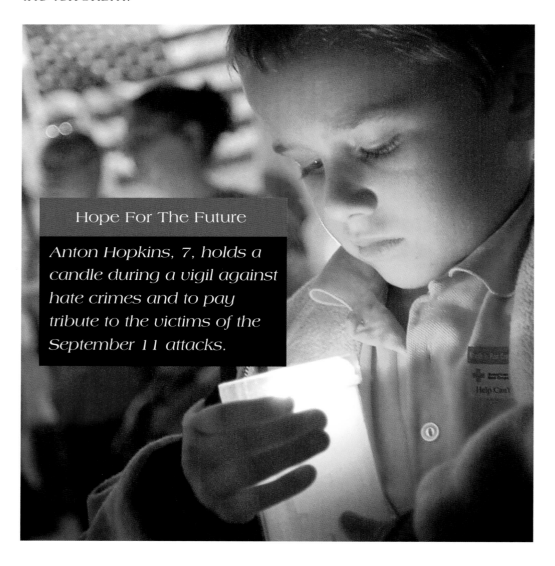

Hope For The Future

Anton Hopkins, 7, holds a candle during a vigil against hate crimes and to pay tribute to the victims of the September 11 attacks.

Paying Respects

New York City Mayor Rudolph Giuliani at a ceremony marking the three-month anniversary of the September 11 attacks.

Honoring Those Lost

The American flag is held over the ice before the start of an NHL hockey game in honor of the victims of the September 11 attacks.

Mayor Giuliani said, "In the name of all of those that we lost here—our heroes, the firefighters, the police officers, the emergency workers, the citizens going about their lives trying to pursue in their way the American dream, all of whom are heroes—we remember them, we will always remember them, and to them we will dedicate the rebuilding of New York and make certain that we do not allow the terrorists in any way to break our spirit. Instead, they have emboldened it."

Thousands of memorial Web sites were created where people could congregate in spite of travel restrictions and other

limitations. People were able to communicate globally, donate money, and mourn the loss of loved ones.

For months and years to come, memorials will be built to honor the heroism displayed on September 11, 2001. One of the largest remaining pieces of the World Trade Center was preserved for future use as part of a memorial. The piece was seen in television, magazine, and newspaper pictures from Ground Zero. Many families of the victims expressed an interest in having a memorial at the site of the World Trade Center as a place to mourn.

Mementos

Firefighting gear from Australia and Indiana are part of a memorial outside a fire station in New York City.

How You Can Help

THERE ARE MANY WAYS PEOPLE OF ALL AGES can unite and lend a helping hand. People who are 17 years or older and weigh more than 110 pounds can donate blood to the Red Cross, or other local blood banks. Students can make red, white, and blue pins to hand out to friends and family, or exchange with other classes in schools or around the country.

Organize a fundraising event, such as a bake sale, car wash, aluminum can collection, or garage sale, and give the money to one of the charities set up to help victims' family members. Ask that donations to help the relief efforts be given instead of presents for birthdays and holidays. Participate in the Remember the Children Yellow Bow Campaign by donating five dollars to one of the youth organizations involved in the fundraiser to show solidarity as a nation. The waterproof bows should be placed outside as a memorial to those affected by the terrorist attack.

Join the Green Ribbon Campaign that celebrates life, peace, and support for the thousands who lost their lives and the millions who were affected by the tragedy. Support your local police and fire departments by sending cards of appreciation, displaying signs in yards, and delivering cookies for all they do in the community.

Timeline

8:45 A.M.   American Airlines Flight 11 crashes into the North Tower of the World Trade Center, setting it on fire.

9:03 A.M.   United Airlines Flight 175 slams into the South Tower of the World Trade Center, setting it on fire as well.

9:30 A.M.   President George W. Bush announces that the nation has suffered a terrorist attack.

9:40 A.M.   The Federal Aviation Administration halts all flight operations at all U.S. airports.

9:43 A.M.   American Airlines Flight 77 crashes into the Pentagon.

10:05 A.M.   The South Tower of the World Trade Center collapses.

10:10 A.M.   A portion of the Pentagon collapses.

10:28 A.M.   The North Tower of the World Trade Center collapses.

10:48 A.M.   Police confirm the crash of United Flight 93 in Pennsylvania.

11:02 A.M.   New York Mayor Rudolph Giuliani asks New Yorkers to stay home and orders everyone south of Canal Street to leave the area.

1:04 P.M.   President Bush promises the U.S. will find and punish the people responsible for the attacks.

1:44 P.M.   Aircraft carriers USS *George Washington* and USS *John F. Kennedy* along with five warships leave Norfolk, Virginia, for the New York coast to further protect the area.

4:00 P.M.   U.S. officials say they believe Osama bin Laden is connected to the attacks.

5:20 P.M.   The 47-story Building 7 of the World Trade Center collapses.

7:45 P.M.   New York officials report that nearly 80 police officers and up to 200 firefighters are believed to have been killed during rescue operations.

8:30 P.M.   President Bush addresses the nation.

Where On The Web?

http://www.people.com

In the search box, type "World Trade Center" to find stories and photos about the attack on America on September 11, 2001.

http://teacher.scholastic.com/newszone/specialreports/ under_attack/kids_help.htm

"Kids Make a Difference," a special online issue from Scholastic.

http://www.ci.nyc.ny.us/html/fdny/home.html

The official Fire Department, City of New York (FDNY) Web site.

http://www.ci.nyc.ny.us/html/nypd/home.html

Official site of the New York Police Department.

http://whitehousekids.gov

This site gives information about what kids can do to help the relief efforts in various ways. It is a special site for kids to learn about government and its function.

http://networkforgood.org

Network For Good is an online resource that makes it easier to donate, volunteer, and make more informed decisions about supporting the causes you care about.

Glossary

casualty
A person who is injured or killed in an act of war.

democracy
A government by the people that is ruled by the majority through representation involving free elections.

emigrate
To leave one's place of residence to live in another country.

five-alarm fire
The largest and most dangerous call for help that involves fire department emergency assistance from many stations.

Ground Zero
The point directly above, below, or at which an explosion occurs. After the first tower collapsed, the World Trade Center was referred to as "Ground Zero."

heroism
Acts of great courage, high achievement, and noble qualities that bring to mind extreme adoration and devotion.

memorial
Something that keeps remembrance alive. After the World Trade Center disaster, many memorials around the world commemorated those who died.

nonprofit
Not conducted or maintained for the purpose of making money.

outreach
The extending of services or assistance beyond current or usual situations.

patriotism
Love for or devotion to one's country.

solidarity
Unity as a group that produces or is based on common interests, objectives, and standards.

terrorism
A systematic use of terror as a means to harm or scare others who do not hold true the same political, religious, or cultural practices and beliefs.

vigil
Evening or night devotion or prayer service to honor certain people or a cause.

Index

A

Achitoff-Gray, Niki 12
Afghanistan 12, 19
Agassi, Andre 35
Albuquerque, NM 28
Alvarez, Veronica 12, 13
Alvarez, Victor 12, 13
Amazon.com 9
America: A Tribute to Heroes 31
American Airlines 28, 29
American Forests 9
American Liberty Partnership 9
American Red Cross 7, 12, 13, 24, 25, 29, 35, 43
America's Fund for Afghan Children 12, 19
Anthony, Marc 31
AOL Time Warner 9
Atlanta, GA 28
Auction for America 9, 35

B

Backstreet Boys 32
Bahrain 20
Baskin, Julia 12
Berlin, Irving 5
Berra, Yogi 35
Big 12 Conference 35
Big Ten Conference 35
Binghamton, NY 13
Bon Jovi 32
Boston, MA 28
British Red Cross 24
Buckingham Palace 25
Bullock, Sandra 35
Bush, George W. 12, 19, 20, 24, 37

C

Canada 24
Canada Loves New York 24
Canadians Care 24
Cannondale 29
Carey, Jim 35
Carnegie Hall 32
Cassato, David 38
Chicago, IL 23
Cisco Systems 9
City University of New York 16
Civil War 11
Clapton, Eric 32
Clooney, George 31
Columbia, S.C. 11
Concert for the Americas 32
Congress, U.S. 19
Cosby, Bill 32
Cross-Cultural Solutions 9
Cruise, Tom 31
Cuba 24

D

Dallas, TX 28
Davenport, Lindsay 35
Department of the Treasury, U.S. 19
Dr. Dre 35
Dubai 25

E

eBay 9, 35
Egypt 20
Ellis Island, NY 29
Emergency Medical Services Command 15
Europe 24, 37
European Union 24

F

Farm Aid 2001 35
Ferrell, Will 32
Flag Across America 28
Flight 11 28
Flight 175 28
Fort Myers, FL 23
France 24
Friendship Through Education 20

G

Giuliani, Rudolph 16, 38, 40
Great Britain 25
Green Ribbon Campaign 43
Ground Zero 7, 9, 13, 29, 32, 38, 41

H

Hanks, Tom 31
Hawn, Goldie 31
Hungary 24

I

International Association of Fire Fighters 15
Iran 24
Islam 20
Israel 24
Italy 24

J

Jackson, Michael 35
Jagger, Mick 32
Jansen, John D. 11
Japan 24
John, Elton 32
John Paul II, Pope 24

K

Kansas City, KS 29
Kinkade, Thomas 27
Kirkland, Jack 12
KMBC-TV 29
Knights of Columbus 29

L

Labelle, Patti 35
Las Vegas, NV 23
Latifah, Queen 35
Lauper, Cyndi 31
Lennon, John 31
Libya 24
Lilly Endowment 9
Liverpool, England 32
London, England 25, 32
Los Angeles, CA 28, 29, 32
Los Angeles International Airport 28
Lynrd Skynrd 32

M

Mackall, Abena 12
Maktoum, Sheikh Mohammed al 25
Madison Square Garden 32
Manhattan, NY 12, 13, 37
Matthews, Dave 31
McCartney, Paul 32
Merchant, Natalie 31
Microsoft Corporation 9
Minneapolis, MN 29

N

NATO 24
NBA 35
Nelson, Willie 35
New Orleans, LA 29
New York 7, 8, 9, 11, 12, 13, 15, 16, 20, 24, 25, 28, 29, 31, 32, 38, 40
New York Community Trust 8
New York Fire Department 32, 38
New York Firefighters 9-11 Disaster Relief Fund 15
New York Police Department 32
New York Police and Fire Widow and Children Benefit 32
New York Times 9/11 Neediest Fund 12
NFL 35
North Tower 12

O

Oceanside Middle School 12
O'Donnell, Rosie 35
Oklahoma City, OK 28
O'Neal, Shaquille 35
Ono, Yoko 31

P

Pakistan 20, 24
Pataki, George 16
Pentagon 27
Phoenix, AZ 28
Poland 29
Police Memorial Park 23
Port Authority of New York and New Jersey 15
Potasnik, Joseph 38
Potter, John E. 20
Prescott Valley, AZ 27

Q

Quinn, Colin 32

R

Red Cross 7, 12, 13, 24, 25, 29, 35, 43
Remember the Children Yellow Bow Campaign 43
Roberts, Julia 31, 35
Rodriguez, Taina 12, 13
Ross, Diana 35
Russia 24

S

Salvation Army 7, 27
Sampras, Pete 35
Seinfeld, Jerry 32
September 11 Telethon Fund 35
September 11th Fund 8, 9
Sister Sledge 35
South Carolina 11
Southeastern Conference 35
Spears, Britney 32
Spirit of New York 9
State University of New York 16
Stop & Shop 29
Stuyvesant High School 12
Syria 24

T

Taliban 19
Teens Improving New York (TINY) 12
Temeczko, Joe 29
Tenenbaum, Inez 11
Thank You America 28
The Light of Freedom 27
Turner, Nancy 11
Twin Towers Fund 15, 32

U

U.S. Embassy 24
U.S. Postal Service 20
Union Square 37
United Airlines 28, 29
United Arab Emirates 25
United States 5, 12, 24, 25, 29, 37
United Way of New York 8

W

Wallace, George 32
Washington, D.C. 20, 28, 29
White Knoll Middle School 11
Who, The 32
Williams, Robin 31
Williams, Serena 35
Williams, Venus 35
Woods, Tiger 35
World Financial Center 9
World Trade Center 12, 15, 24, 27, 35, 41
World Trade Center Relief Fund 15
World War II 32
WTC Memorial Quilt 27

Y

Yahoo 9